Out *of* Time

*for those who grieve
and wonder*

a memoir

Victoria Cull

A portion of proceeds from this book will be donated in Nicole's name to Girls Opportunity Alliance, an organization that seeks to empower and educate adolescent girls around the world.

Cover & interior design by Typewriter Creative Co.
Cover & interior photos (excl. p. 13, 37, 55, 95) by Victoria Cull.
Author photo by Carl Cull.
Hourglass in the garden by Volodymyr Chevchuk / Adobe Stock.

ISBN 979-8-218-65828-1 (Paperback)
ISBN 979-8-218-65730-7 (eBook)

Out of Time: For Those Who Grieve and Wonder is a gem that might easily be overlooked as only a personal memoir of grief over the death of a grandchild. But that wouldn't do justice to the way the book moves the reader from her own story to one's own. The loss of a child, be it yours, a grandchild, other family member, or a close friend is as disorienting as it sounds. While the author is a person of faith, this book is for both faith-oriented individuals as well as those who are not. The author and fellow griever writes uniquely from a personal, theological, and therapeutic perspective. She gives her readers full permission to wander through the wilderness of grief without a formulaic approach or tidy answers. Each grief journey is unique and the book graciously allows for and honors our differences as we seek a new equilibrium.

—Rev. Dr. Dawn Lindholm
Chaplain, author, and child loss survivor

Out of Time: For Those Who Grieve and Wonder is a deeply touching testament to the unwavering faith and love that holds us together even during our darkest moments. Written by a woman who has known the pain of loss in its most intimate form, this book tells the story of a grandmother's journey through the unimaginable loss of her precious granddaughter, Nicole. I felt the intergenerational love between Nicole and her grandmother on every page. It's as if Nicole is present with the author, informing the story and urging it forward, taking the reader by the hand and showing us the way. The author not only tells the story of her loss, but she is a conduit in telling Nicole's story - a vibrant teenager navigating her last days, holding her loved ones close as she prepares to let them go.

Having worked with many who have experienced grief, I can say with confidence that this book offers something rare: an authentic unfiltered message of hope for all who grieve, a love letter that freely laments the unfairness of life yet finds safety in the enduring presence of a loving God.

—**Darci Morris,** MSW

For Nicole, of course, whose name means "victory"

time:

the indefinite continued progress of
existence and events in the past, present,
and future, regarded as a whole

wonder:

a feeling of surprise mingled with admiration;
the desire to be curious to know something;
feel doubt

Contents

The Big Life of Nicole Keller

catch a million waves

sing a million songs

laugh a million laughs

make a million friends

dance a million steps

feel a million feels

pray a million prayers

cry a million tears

play a million chords

write a million words

dream a million dreams

break a million hearts

Teach us to number our days that we may get a heart of wisdom.

Psalm 90:12

Introduction

After losing my fifteen year old granddaughter to bone cancer, all of my long held beliefs about who God is were thrown into deep question. I wasn't so angry that I wanted to turn my back on God. I was just confused. Stunned. Adrift. Deeply disappointed. A cocktail of swirling emotions that left me trying desperately to understand how God works.

This part of my family's story does not end the way we'd longed for. It is the story of how I lost my granddaughter and almost lost my faith along with her.

This book is not an account that is all tied up with a pretty bow at the end. I think the truth is always better than fiction, and Nicole was a truth-teller. She faced the hardships that were thrown at her with authenticity. So for me to be anything less than truthful on these pages would be a disservice to the bravery and grace Nicole lived out. It is my hope that through the honest recounting of all the struggles and tears, and yes, so much joy, someone might find their own answers to unanswered questions or at least find some peace through the pain.

This book is about struggle, but it's also about the beautiful life Nicole lived, how she died, and how her faith has inspired me to be courageous enough to ask the hard questions.

This is a small book about a big life.

Chapter One

The First of Three Phone Calls

I t was 7:00 in the morning on July 22, 2008. My husband and I were living in Southern California and were four miles into a thirteen mile hike. When his cell phone rang I immediately knew something was wrong. And my intuition was correct. It was MacKenzie, our then thirty year old daughter, who was pregnant with her first child. As I saw the look of concern on my husband's face as he took in what was being said on the other line, I shifted my body's weight from one foot to the other, anxiety mounting. MacKenzie was telling him that she had been at the hospital since 2:00 a.m. that her placenta was detaching and there was a loss of a lot of blood. It was two and a half weeks too early for this baby to come and it was imperative that we get up to the hospital in Redwood City as soon as possible.

What to do? Our car was parked four miles behind us and we needed to get in it, drive home and get airline reservations and make arrangements for care for our dogs. SO! We started to hitchhike. A kind man picked us up within a few minutes and I remember I shared the back seat with a load of freshly caught fish in a smelly cooler. I felt I really should pay him somehow, so I feebly offered my crumbled granola bar as payment. (I think he declined.)

We made it home, took care of the dogs, got on a plane, and arrived in plenty of time to greet our brand new healthy grand baby girl. At the hospital, I settled down and prepared myself before entering the room where Nicole was cradled in her smiling mama's arms. What I was not prepared for was how the next fifteen years and five months would impact me, change my life and my heart forever now that I had Nicole in my life.

And so the journey began. Because my husband and I were both retired, I was able to drive up to Redwood City often to help my daughter and to care for this new little wonder. I remember how, like many parents and grandparents of newborns, I would just stare into her face for long minutes, in awe of each little pucker of her lips or twitch of her little sleeping eyes. Charles Dickens was so right when he wrote, "They come to us so fresh from God." I am glad I didn't know that fifteen years hence I could repeat this experience of staring with love into the face of this child. But this time she would be semiconscious and making her way toward her heavenly home.

LOVE

is wut

we nyd

Nicole Keller, age 5

Chapter Two

Early Years

After Nicole was born it soon became apparent to me that something would have to be done about all these miles that separated us. I would often drive up from San Diego to my daughter's home near San Francisco to help out with the new baby. After spending several days and it was time for me to go back home, I would rise early in the dark of the morning without saying any goodbyes. I'd sneak out the door, drive down highway 5 with the rising sun glowing through the left hand window of my car and weep all the way to Los Angeles.

It wasn't long before my husband and I found a sweet little cottage on the central coast of California, one block back from a cliff that overlooks the grandeur of the Pacific Ocean. Our home is called "The Sea Rose" and came complete with a bunk room that would become the setting for many happy sleepovers for all of our grandchildren.

Daughter Melissa had brought little cousin Even into the world four months prior. Now the next four years would be full to the brim with the birth of one grandchild after another, six in all. Watching my grandchildren grow up has been the joy of my life. Being a grandmother affords you a do-over - ways to do better with these little ones when you are older, wiser and more patient than when you were raising your own kids. Grandparents are an extra pair hands when needed and a source of encouragement when parenting is a challenge. I've heard it said, "Grandparents are parents with sprinkles." Two scenes: In number one scene I am a harried and hurried young mother making pancakes for my little girls. Me: "Hurry up and eat and stop fooling around." In number two scene I am Mimi, the doting grandmother. Me: "Good morning my darlings. Would you like your pancakes cut into stars with a dusting of powdered sugar?"

I guess every family has those little tales they tell a child about what they were like when they were small, anecdotes that become part of the family's folklore, little stories that make up the big story of who a family is. Stories that cement the child's place in the family and make them feel special. Nicole lived in such a way that it is easy to remember so many of the funny and poignant things she said and did when she was little. Still, I know there are so many little scenarios lost to time. Things that seemed inconsequential at the time but that now I would give anything to have back.

She was a precocious child in every way. Bright, curious about everything, always wanting to be a part of conversations that adults were having. And when she wasn't included she'd eavesdrop. Once I was talking about one of those two seater bikes where there is an extension on the back for a child to ride. "Nicole, I said. Wouldn't that be fun for us?" And she replied, "Yes, I'll sit in the front."

One day another granddaughter was riding with me *on the back* of said bicycle. She was small and frightened. Her mom, my daughter Courtney, kept saying, "Jaelyn! Jaelyn! Trust Mimi! Trust Mimi!"

Wobbling along and new to this grandmothering business, I was struck by this command Courtney was giving her daughter. "Trust Mimi! " What a weighty thing to hold in your grasp. I wanted then and now to always live up to that - to be a good and trustworthy grandmother.

Thanks to her mom, MacKenzie, Nicole was an early student of the Bible. Once when she was maybe two years old I went to visit her and when I entered the house there was Nicole running around in circles. Around and around she went. "Nicole! I said. What are you doing?" She told me between laps, "I'm running away from God!" Apparently her mom had just read her the story of Jonah and the whale and how Jonah didn't want to comply with God's wishes and was "running away from God." (Jonah 1:1-3) In her life, thankfully Nicole never did consciously make a choice to run away from God and despite much hardship, she was always full of his love.

If life on Planet Earth is a school for being human, Nicole even at age five, was a teacher. Her mom walked into the playroom one day and on her little easel she had written:

LOVE

is wut

we nyd

Seems like she had it figured out already. An early awakening.

When Nicole was small she loved to read and be read to. Such a thoughtful child, she would often pick out books from her school library that she thought I would enjoy and bring them home to me. She loved her little sister Natalie fiercely but was often at loggerheads with her, Nicole trying to have her own space and making sure Natalie knew who was boss. This of course was very frustrating for Natalie and one incident was recorded in MacKenzie's journal: When Nicole was only seven years old she and Natalie were having a skirmish and Nicole had barricaded herself in the bathroom. When her mom said, "Nicole, your sister is trying to get your attention!" Nicole said, "I know! That is why I am writing a non-fiction book on how to deal with a sister!" It makes me wonder if Nicole might have gone on to become a talented writer.

In the sixth grade Nicole was voted "The Classmate Most Likely to be a Friend", and one of Nicole's attributes that was sited was, "She listens."

Empathic, compassionate, once when Nicole and her mom

were volunteering in the church nursery the baby under their care began to cry - and Nicole cried too!

I chuckled when I read what one of Nicole's elementary school teachers wrote as a part of her evaluation:

Nicole is diligent, bright and respectful. She is above grade level in all academic areas, but still she continues to work hard and challenge herself. She takes great care and thoughtfulness in all she does. Nicole has recently become distracted by classmates and is eager to demonstrate her sense of humor. We talked about this and when there might be a more appropriate time for her to showcase her wit.

It seemed Nicole's time at her Auntie Courtney's academic preschool was paying off. And she was a well-rounded, happy girl.

Through the years Nicole's cousins were a huge part of her life. Probably nothing makes a grandmother happier than to see her children's children love each other. From the beginning my West Coast grandkids: Nicole, Natalie, Jaelyn and Nathanial were a matched set. When I remember these days from the past, it's as though I have a movie playing in my head and I can see them: they are spending hours playing dress-up, the big girls dressing little Nathaniel up too; all four kids riding bikes around Auntie Courtney's neighborhood; all of the sound and fury of them making up silly plays to perform for the adults.

Simple things. Just being together. These cousins celebrated every single Christmas together- church on Christmas Eve, then in the morning always a riot of colorful wrapping paper and gifts and warm laughter and our traditional family Christmas Kringle bread. There are too many memories to recount.

One of the benefits of keeping a journal or diary is that sometimes small tender moments are recorded, moments that would otherwise be lost to time and overtaken by what we perceive to be the big things in life. One such scenario is this - something I wrote marking the beginning of Spring:

spring break weekend, April 6, 2019

Natalie climbed a tree today and hollered down, "Mom, come quick!" She had discovered a bird's nest with two azure blue eggs. I'm so glad she experienced this joy! Spring is definitely in the air and I could hear the little chirping coming from the tree limbs as we walked to the park. Later on a cozy evening with Courtney and MacKenzie doing that dance cooks do in the kitchen while they move around each other, making dinner. We had music playing in the background and there were four sweet cousins playing nearby.

The days follow one after another and take their places in the past and our little stories find their place within the big one. Journaling reveals that the little things are really the big things.

Our family has been blessed to be able to take many amazing trips together and it was wonderful when the East Coast grandkids, Even and Ilse, could join in too: Hawaii, Mexico, Lake Tahoe, Boston, New York, Palm Springs - and the grandchildren were always the focal point for me. Traveling with the kids in the backseat, looking in the rearview mirror and seeing Nicole helping Nathaniel sound out words in a book. Fond memories of the six kids running a foot race, splashing in the ocean, Natalie always coming up with some mischief. And as the kids became adolescents, Jaelyn and Nicole spending hours on the phone together, trading secrets, trying to figure out life. Jaelyn has since written a poem for Nicole and described the bond that she and Nicole developed over the years. The poem beautifully expresses how Nicole had been her rock, her shining star, and that Jaelyn had found a home in her. I hope that Nicole can now see her cousin Nathaniel (who was like a little brother to her) transformed into a tall athletic boy burning up the basketball court. This cousin time was foundational to Nicole's happy childhood, a time that will never be lost, even now. Because love never dies.

Chapter Three

A Grandmother's Story

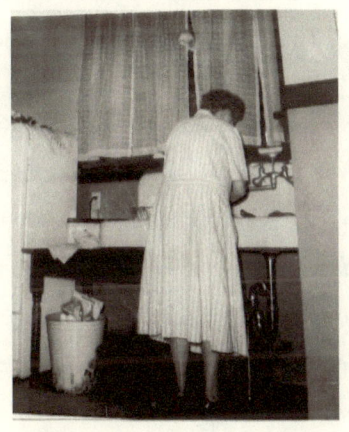

T his is Nicole's story, told by me, her grandmother. But it's also my story and my daughters' stories and their children's stories. Because we are inextricably linked, body and soul. Psalm 139 says, "You knit me together in my mother's womb." (See Appendix B)

And now I know these words are more than poetic language. A few years ago I read about the phenomenon of microchimerism. It is when fetal cells pass through the placenta and into the mother's body and the cells intermix. This is called fetal-maternal microchimerism. Mother and child carry parts of each other. And the cells can remain for decades in the bodies after they are passed down from a woman to her child to her grandchild.[1] In an article titled "Children's Cells Live on in Mothers" author Laura Sanders explains further:

> *Way back when you and your mom shared a body, your cells mingled. Her cells slipped into your body and your cells circled back into her. This process, called fetal-maternal microchimerism, turns both mother and child into chimeras harboring little pieces of each other. Cells from my daughters are knitted into my body and bones and brain. I also carry cells from my mom, and quite possibly from my grandma.*[2]

Microchimerism illuminates our God as the great designer, creator, and artist that he is.

Richard Rohr has some beautiful words to say in this regard. He says,

> *Once a woman has carried her baby inside for nine months and brought it forth….she knows the mystery of transformation at a cellular level. She knows it intuitively, yet she usually cannot verbalize it, nor does she need to. She just holds it at deeper level of consciousness. She knows something about mystery, about miracles, about transformation that men will never know… The feminine body can be seen as a cauldron of transformation. Her body turns things into other things- turns an act of love into a perfect little child. Yet, in her heart, she knows she did not do it. All she had to do was wait and eat well, to believe and to hope for nine months. This gives a woman very special access to understanding spirituality as transformation- if she is able to listen to her own experience and her own body.[3]*

Our bodies, minds and spirits are inseparable. The psychiatrist Carl Jung said, *"Every mother contains her daughter in herself, and every daughter her mother, and every mother extends backwards through her mother and forward into her daughter."*

Virginia Wolfe also comments: *"Our daughters and our granddaughters belong to each other, linking past and future. We live backwards through our mothers and forward through our daughters."*

This is not to say that if Nicole's mom, MacKenzie, told Nicole's story it would be exactly the same view as mine. Grandmothers have their own filters, their own way of seeing things in regards to their grandchildren.

I love the very word "grandmother". Being a grandmother is the best thing I've ever been and has brought me more joy than any other experience in my life. My love for each of my grandchildren sits way down deep in my soul.

I was blessed with a grandmother who I would often hear humming hymns - "What a Friend We Have in Jesus" comes to mind- as she worked in the kitchen. There she would stand at her work, tight lipped and stern, wearing a printed house dress and flowered bib apron, heavy stockings and black clunky shoes, hair held severely in place by a number of bobby pins.

I was a willful child. I remember there were times when I was ill and my fever would spike, quickly escalating into the 104 territory so it was important that I get some aspirin in my system. When I refused to take the aspirin my mom offered me she would try to trick me into taking it by dissolving it in a bottle of 7up. But I could see the detritus of the pill at the bottom of the bottle and would refuse to drink it. Once when I was not ill, but just wanted to enjoy a bottled soda (yes, children drank those in those days) I was feeling suspicious that maybe somehow someone had snuck an offending pill in there. After a back and forth with my mom, my older brother, and my older sister who each assured me there was no pill in the soda I was still not convinced. My mom's advice? Ask Grandma. Because she doesn't lie. So my very small mind extrapolated two things about grandmas: one: they see Jesus as their friend and, two: they can be counted on to always tell you the truth. My grandma was a staunch Lutheran and she and my mom raised us three kids to believe in the importance and power of prayer. But more about that later.

I'm delighted to say that grandmas get some special attention in the Bible. Paul, in his letter to his companion Timothy, encourages him when he writes,

> *I am reminded of your sincere faith, which first lived in your grandmother Lois and in your mother Eunice and I am persuaded now lives in you also. (2 Timothy 1:5)*

Grandmas matter. My heart is always touched when I read how the saga of Ruth played out after she had followed her mother-in-law Naomi back to Bethlehem. When Ruth ultimately gave birth to her son, grandmother Naomi "took the child in her arms and cared for him" (Ruth 4:16) This child was cared for by three strong women: mother Ruth, and grandmothers Naomi and Rahab- and they all became part of the lineage of Jesus.

Kat Armas in her book *Abuelita Faith* speaks about the wisdom of her grandmother, her abuela, and how she learned so much through this wise old women's "kitchen theology". These were life lessons that could only come from a woman who had lived through a lot and seen a few things....feet that had walked hard paths. Kat Armas points out that giants like Cesar Chavez and Martin Luther King, Jr. were deeply influenced by their grandmothers.[4] I humbly seek to be a part of this community, guiding my grandkids along the way.

I know I was a sounding board for Nicole when things got hard and she knew I was cheering her on every step of the way. Nicole was my friend but she showed me respect and honored my role as her grandmother. We loved each other well. But now, as we shall see at the end of Nicole's story here on earth, the whole thing became backwards. The order of things was disrupted and flipped. I was supposed to be Nicole's abuela, her strong, wise, and staid grandmother. And Nicole was supposed gain strength from me in order that she might move on and live a long and full life long after I had passed away. Nicole, the beautiful, full grown woman and possibly wife and mother, was supposed to tell stories about her times with me, her grandmother, and how these experiences informed her thinking, her theology, her life. In this upside down world, now Nicole is my ancestor - not the other way around.

Now, I believe, Nicole is the one blazing the sacred trail, alive somewhere I've never been. She is the one with the answers. Here on Planet Earth, at fifteen years old, Nicole's pure and intuitive heart often had the right answers. How much more true this must be now from where she sits out in eternity. This I know is true: she and I are forever tethered to each other across time and space no matter our familial relationship to each other.

Chapter Four

Take These Broken Wings and Learn to Fly

T oward the end of her life Nicole and I were meeting regularly to study the Bible together, seeking comfort and answers to questions that would never have an answer. Nicole was doing her soul work, facing head on the challenges she had been given. I know she did not believe that her cancer was part of God's plan. Nicole was a truth-teller and because she faced life with authenticity she was able to be genuine in her interactions with others and we had some good, honest discussions. Once, in the midst of all of her medical procedures, we were discussing sorrow and how when you experience sorrow, your heart is broken open and how, at best, it can then be open to floodgates of love and compassion. She looked at me with her sad and beautiful eyes and said, "Mimi, I've had a lot of sorrow in my life."

Somewhere in a journal entry from long ago I had written a slogan that sounds like it came from a Hallmark card. Amidst my colorful doodles of cheery flowers it says, "She loved life and it loved her right back." Right now it didn't feel like life was loving either one of us right back. Life had thrown Nicole a wicked curve ball that struck with deadly force.

Nicole, like so many adolescent girls, struggled through seventh grade. But I think because she was an especially sensitive girl she had a rougher time than most. She counted on the goodness of people and was often deeply hurt and disappointed. I can only say never underestimate the desire for a seventh girl to fit in and have community and never underestimate the herd mentality of some of that population.

But seventh grade mercifully came to an end and it wasn't long before we could see that something beautiful was about to unfold with the help of a girl named Scarlett. She and Nicole had been peripheral friends but one day this beautiful, tall, confident, open faced girl strode up to MacKenzie and said, "Hi. I'm Scarlett. I'm Nicole's new best friend. You're going to be seeing a lot of me."

After that things got better. Nicole was still skittish and afraid to trust. But Scarlett came barreling into her life, loving her, making her laugh again and enveloping Nicole into her friend group, a bunch of kids who were healthy, open, full of life, humor, and goodwill.

Nicole began playing her guitar more and one of the songs she was teaching herself was "Blackbird" by the Beatles. Even with wings that had been broken, our girl was learning to fly again, coming back to her center.

She began volunteering for an organization called Teen Kitchen where she would go each week and help prepare food to be taken to people who couldn't leave their homes. She blossomed knowing that she was helping others and she reveled in the discipline of it - loved it that the volunteers had to say, "Yes Chef!" when given some direction.

Fully immersed in a healthy friend group, living a life of purpose, Nicole found her shining self again and there were many magical times ahead.

Chapter Five

The Second of
Three Phone Calls

Unfortunately, at the beginning of her freshman year, just as things were going so well, Nicole began to complain of pain in her right knee. At first we though it was just "growing pains" or more specifically Osgood Schlatter's Disease, an ailment common in adolescents during growth spurts. But MacKenzie wisely quickly pursued more information and after a series of X-rays, MRI's, and finally a biopsy, a pediatric oncologist gave MacKenzie the devastating news that it was osteosarcoma. There was cancer in her femur. It was considered high grade and chemo would need to start immediately. The pediatric oncologist further explained that even though this type of of cancer only occurs in one out of 500,000 people, it is the most common pediatric cancer and that everything looked standard and would be treated as such. PET and CT scans assured us that the cancer was contained to her leg. Next up: inserting a port in Nicole's chest where the chemo drug would be administered over the next nine months, and three months hence surgery to replace the cancerous bone with an internal prosthetic bone.

This was the second time in my life when my husband's cell phone rang and I huddled next to him to hear news that was scary but this time it felt devastating. We were all stunned but hopeful and ready to take this on to support Nicole, her mom, and sister Natalie any way that we could. God was on our side. We were sure of it.

Chapter Six

Chemo and More Chemo

E very single day over the next year brought a new challenge. There were days filled with hope and days filled with anxiety and deep despair. Our lives, especially Nicole's and MacKenzie's lives, became a blur of one doctor appointment after another, hospital stays, chemo infusions, blood transfusions, two surgeries, and constant battles with pain and nausea.

My daughter, it seemed, became super human and met each challenge with strength and faith and good humor. And this, of course, encouraged and bolstered Nicole. I could write a whole separate book about this wonder of a daughter. It's impossible to convey in words how tenderly she cared for and tended to Nicole through it all….and to try and do so would be an invasion of the sacred space they shared. Mack's deep love for her girl, and her deep faith, trust, and eternal hope were amazing to witness. She would quickly tell you that all of her strength came from God, and that she was driven by an unexplainable power beyond herself.

Almost immediately after she was diagnosed Nicole went to her friend's house and shaved her head, pre-empting the inevitable. Over the next months she received literally hundreds of gifts: beanies, blankets, socks (oh so many socks) meals, baked goods, candy, and best of all -letters of love and encouragement.

The protocol for treating Nicole's cancer was a complicated, weighty, and ugly process.

I remember the first time I set foot in the pediatric oncology ward where she had just been admitted. Just typing those words puts ice in my veins. I felt like a horse who was balking. I wanted to firmly plant my feet and not go forward to a place that seemed a complete contradiction of what a childhood should look like. Try as they might to create a cheery and healing space it was still a cancer ward. For children. Who may or may not live. None of this made sense.

Nicole entered the hospital each month for chemo infusions and would spend three to four nights there at a time. There would ultimately be 92 overnights in all for this part of her treatment. MacKenzie, of course, spent most of these days and nights in the hospital with her but her sister Courtney and I took over some times too to give Mack a break and also so she could spend time with little sister Natalie.

Auntie Courtney pitched in with all the love and strength she could muster. While Nicole slept, Courtney would spend hours hovering over her bed, singing a prayerful song for her. Seeking heaven, begging God for a miracle healing.

When it was my turn to help with Nicole we would drive to the hospital, get her checked in and within a few hours the nurse would come in and hook her up to the chemo bag which at first felt like a bag of scary pure poison but became, in our minds, Nicole's ticket to restored health.

Nicole would spend much of the time sleeping, ordering food, and most of all making friends with the nurses. Always thinking of others and curious about others' life stories, Nicole would ask questions about their families, wanting to know how *they* were doing. Many of the nurses would tell MacKenzie that the tables were turned - at the end of their shifts they often felt that Nicole had lifted their spirits and had helped them more than they helped her, a bright spot in their days. Nicole developed sweet relationships with several nurses. Julie, a consistent source of encouragement, often prayed with Nicole and MacKenzie. And, understanding Nicole's love of music, she gifted Nicole all of her dad's old vinyl records. Becky, a traveling nurse who wasn't even assigned to Nicole's care, heard other nurses talking about Nicole and soon came to meet her. Sweet Becky with her lilting warm southern accent and kind ways. These angel nurses made the unbearable bearable.

One of the nurses who was named Theresa, who Nicole called "Mama T", was especially wonderful to Nicole. This older, petite, gentle Vietnamese-American, Christian woman was exactly what Nicole needed as the chemo dripped, and the nausea and pain and discouragement were too much. MacKenzie recorded word for word in her journal what Mama T would say to Nicole:

Mama T would take Nicole's face into her hands and say, "You gonna be ok Baby. God is with you. And I will take care of you while you are here. It's a long hard road but you gonna be ok. You are strong. If you feel sad then you cry. It is ok. But then you pick yourself up and go. God makes you strong, Baby. You can do hard things. God is always with you, no matter what. Even in the dark times. You can do this."

Each scene played out in this kind of parallel universe of a hospital ward with its alien scents, artificial lighting, and quiet voices. Nicole was making the best of it, finding things to laugh at, making connections with those around her, and at times head bowed in prayer, trusting that her God and the adults in her life were doing what was best for her.

Sleeping on the fold out bed in her room, the nights were filled with the constant beeping of the machines. The nurses would come in often and let's just say some were quieter than others. Because Nicole had to remain on the IV bag, I would get up with her several times in the night and help her drag the IV pole to the bathroom, wait, and then help her back to bed. If it sounds like I'm complaining, I am not. Weirdly, these were the most profound moments of my life and to say

I wouldn't trade them for anything would be ridiculous but suffice to say that I have never felt more spiritually connected in such a unique way to someone I love so dearly.

The best part was, after several days, when the labs showed that her body had cleared the chemo, we were ready to go home. These are the moments I will hold in my my heart forever.

Before cancer struck Nicole and I used to love to get a Starbucks coffee (I still have her standard order on my phone: grande light iced chai with sugar free vanilla) and drive around Paradise Point in Santa Cruz and take in the ocean and listen to music. She was a talented musician in her own rite and could harmonize and pick out chords that I didn't recognize. So on these nights after she was discharged very late at night and so so happy to be going home (one more chemo treatment down and one step closer to restored health we imagined) I would get Nicole into the wheelchair and I would push her happily, crazily, speedily down the hospital halls, into the elevator, out to my car and whoosh! We would drive through the dark night over the mountainous Highway 17 and Nicole would call up songs on the sound system in my car - The Beatles, The Smiths, Elvis, Jack Johnson, and even Etta James and Billy Holiday. We would laugh and sing at the top of our lungs all the way home. Once we were still laughing loudly as we walked in the door of her home, disturbing the sleep of MacKenzie and little sister Natalie and probably the neighbors. Mack scowled at me and rolled her eyes but I know she was delighted to have her girl home again and safe and loved and happy. This was such a bright spot amid all of the pain and uncertainty.

Chapter Seven

Tolling Bell

Here is, in part, what Nicole wrote in her journal on Good Friday, April 7, 2023. A prayerful letter to God just as her chemo treatments were finally coming to an end:

> *Hello Abba! Hello Jesus! Hello My Father, Glory to the Shining Remover of Darkness! Today is a very important day. My brain cannot comprehend, words cannot describe, there is no understanding of how much you love me; love us. Jesus, you are my hero. You are my comfort, you are holy and you are love. Thank you. Today I had my LAST EVER chemo treatment. On such an (already) important day -Good Friday. I am almost DONE. DONE might just be my new favorite word. This is all coming true- coming to an end. Thank you Lord. This chapter of my life is concluding. Thank you for the character development and progress in my faith and relationship with you. It is well with my soul. I hate cancer but I love you. Jesus you saved me. I've seen your face- Jesus you are my best, my most true friend. You are my hero. Almost DONE. In Jesus's precious name. Amen.*

My heart is so full, so grieved, when I see how vulnerable, how trusting, how full of love, gratitude, faith, and hope this child was.

And so after all of these months of treatment, Nicole finished her very last chemo infusion. There would be further scans and appointments just to make sure the cancer was gone, but at this point we all felt the very worst was behind us.

Tradition holds that after the cancer patient receives his or her last treatment, all of the caregivers in the hospital would line up down the hall. The patient would be pushed down the hall in a wheelchair to the cheers and whoops of everyone. A joyous parade. Then the patient would ring a bell that was placed near the nurses' station, signifying healing and health and a battle won. Here is what I wrote in my journal:

On May 3, 2023, after 92 total nights in the hospital since September, at approximately 10:30 p.m., to the cheers of all of her faithful nurses, our Nicole rang that bell and we, her family, escorted her out of the building. It's a wrap. Our God is good.

Chapter Eight

Precious Days

I n the middle of all of this Nicole attended her school's winter formal with her friend group. Mack invited seven girls to come to their home and get ready for this big occasion. It was several hours of a mixture of make-up applications, hair styling, trying on and rejecting and accepting various dresses and shoes. Girls being girls. In the end, her sweet bald head covered with a beanie and her little dress as short and crazy as style dictated, off they all went and she danced the night away.

As the weeks went on life could feel pretty normal. Nicole went to school when she felt up to it and when all of her many doctor appointments didn't get in the way.

Outside of school, Nicole was preparing for the big day when she would turn sixteen -so excited at the prospect of getting her driver's license. Her mom and a family friend were letting her drive in unpopulated areas - quiet streets and parking lots. She was learning a lot and was liberal in her advice to me regarding my own driving now that she was becoming an expert.

One day Nicole and her friends were walking around the village of a local surfer town and browsing through stores. Nicole had a deep dark scar on her leg that went from the inside of her knee all the way up her thigh - a reminder of two painful surgeries to replace the cancerous bone in her leg. A boy in one of the stores noticed and said, "Dude, what happened?" To which Nicole replied, "A shark got me."

At some point over the next few months, the girls decided it would be a great idea to have matching tattoos. So Scarlett got out her magic ingredients and Nicole, Scarlett, Ava, and Julia each came away with a tiny heart tattoo on her ankle.

That summer we celebrated Nicole's fifteenth birthday. I posted a picture of her blowing out the candles with the caption: "Happy birthday Brave One. May you have many more." Daughter Melissa and family came from the East Coast and we celebrated cousin Ilse's birthday and Poppa's (my husband/ Nicole's grandfather) too. The six grandkids played a modified game of stick ball down on the beach, using Nicole's crutch as a bat. Summers are festive times where we live. A local restaurant hosts barbecues on the beach with a live band and the whole family went. Uncle Montique carried Nicole on his back from the car because the sand was too deep for Nic to navigate on her crutches. Our family felt like a team and I was filled with gratitude.

Nicole and her Poppa had a special code. Nicole loved to come to our house and even as a teenager would often ask to spend the night in the bunk room that was set up for the grandkids' visits. Through the years, after each visit, when it was time for her to go home Nicole and her Poppa would both always pause, look each other in the eye and say, "Don't forget!" (An unspoken I love you.)

Now Poppa took on a new role and had a new nickname for Nicole. He called her "Nails" as in "tough as". He became Nicole's unofficial physical therapist. Nicole even changed his name in her contacts to read "Personal Trainer". He would go to Nicole's home three times a week and work with her. When they would go to the gym Poppa made it known that Nicole had a big love for Elvis and the guy at the front desk would see her in the parking lot, limping or hobbling on crutches towards the door and he would quickly put on an Elvis song, a happy greeting for our girl. Nicole's big smile and bigger heart drew people to her. Her kindness was contagious.

These precious weeks were full of hope. Even though she still had a number of doctor appointments and lots of physical therapy, our girl was going to be just fine and we were all pouring as much love into her as we could.

Chapter Nine

The Third and Final Phone Call

This will be the hardest chapter to write because the news my husband and I received this time threw us into an abyss. I remember where I was sitting - in the living room of our home - and I don't remember whose phone rang, my husband's or mine, but I do remember with clarity that Mack was calling from the hospital and she reported that Nic had gone in for her three month scan and the oncologist had called them into his office to say that the cancer had metastasized to her spine. I remember standing up and pacing the floor and raging at God: "What kind of God lets a fifteen year old child die?" And ranting that our family will never be the same and that the hole in our family that Nicole would leave would be enormous.

The date was September 3, 2023 and we didn't know it yet but we'd have only three more months with our girl.

The next day my husband and I accompanied Mack and Nicole to another meeting with the pediatric oncologist. We four sat awkwardly in a stark room at a long table lit by florescent bulbs. Also present was a palliative care nurse and a social worker. Someone came in and looked at us and asked brightly, "So how are you doing now?" ...or something inane like that and I just stared at her while my husband replied, "I think we are just numb." The doctor was late. When he came in he began to speak in a detached voice with words that I couldn't understand because I felt like my head was under water and then he proceeded to go through some kind of slide show whose contents I cannot recall. Nicole left the room.

A few days later the title page of my journal said:

Life as we knew it is now over.

I'm angry today. I hate cancer. I hate hospitals. I hate Dr. _'s eyes with no kindness in them. I hate what this is doing to Nicole, Mack, and Natalie. I cannot bear it. I used to tell my daughters when they were small when they'd have a close call like stepping off a curb too soon or some typical reckless behavior of a child, "If anything ever happened to you I'd never be happy again." And it <u>was</u> true. And now it <u>is</u> true. I will live, but I will never be happy again. I am numb; I am jumpy; I am desolate. I am angry. The sadness is so deep and scary I'm afraid to touch it. I am confused. I cannot ask WHY or I will split apart. I cannot protect Nicole. I cannot protect my family from this pain.

I had always loved that quote by Frederick Buechner: "Here is the world. Terrible and beautiful things will happen. Don't be afraid." Well now I was afraid. Very. Very Afraid.

The time remaining felt like we were all living out of reality. I could not find the words to pray to a God I no longer trusted. Brave Nicole just didn't want to discuss her death and I remember, as time was winding down for her, sitting across from her at one of our favorite restaurants where I used to take her to pancakes before school on Wednesdays. I told her that I'd take this cancer from her in an instant if I could. "Give it to me! I will bear it for you!" I said. We looked into each others' dry eyes and I said, "I'd cry with you now, but I'm afraid I'd never be able to stop." Nicole replied that she felt the same way. And so it went. Day to day trying to live but knowing she was dying. That day I took her back to my house. She was in so much pain. It was so hard to get the drugs right. I wanted so much to tell her brighter days were ahead, but we both knew that was a lie. I settled her on the sofa with a heating pad and more meds and lay down beside her, staying close the whole morning, making her warm cups of Ovaltine, loving her.

Chapter Ten

God is Not my Heavenly Bell Hop

P rayer is in my DNA. My grandmother and my mother believed in the power of prayer and encouraged me to pray.

When I was six or seven years old I'd ride my bike down the street to visit my friends. Peddling away, I'd be praying that they would be home. Literally praying that God would arrange it so that they would be there. I remember wondering in my little child mind if God would magically make them appear for me. What if they were at the grandparents' house? Or at the store? Or just anywhere else? Even then my theology was at work. I had to admit to my small self that this prayer was probably worthless and that God probably didn't operate that way.

But still through the years I continued to pray prayers much like these out of my childlike trust that God would answer me. God please help me pass this test in school. God please let that cute boy in third period ask me out. Maybe prayers like these would have been better: (But I didn't know it then and I'm just learning it now) God, just be in this with me; If my friends are home please just be there too; God, please help me to quiet my mind so that I can do my best on this test; God, help me to want what you want.

Later, as an adult, anytime I'd see someone in distress on the freeway, or an ambulance rushing by, a child crying, a couple arguing, I would begin to pray - sometimes aloud - that all would be well with these people, asking my God, my trusted Father, to intervene. All of my life I have energetically joined prayer teams. When someone asked me to pray for them I'd do it. And then I'd follow up to see how that person was getting on. I've never been a shallow "thoughts and prayers" kind of Christian. If you needed prayer, I was your girl.

It's easy to trust God when things are going smoothly, when you think you can see evidence of his grace. A relationship is healed and you give him credit. The surgery is a success or the cancer is defeated and you thank him. But trust can soon turn into bitterness and despair when the divorce is finalized, the surgery is not a success, the cancer metastasizes.

It takes humility to pray, to admit you don't have all of the answers. That you are not in control and that you cannot do it alone. I know I'm not God, as he reminded Job in the midst of Job's terrible tribulations:

Where were you when I laid the earth's foundations? Tell me if you know. Who set its measurements? Surely you know. Who stretched a measuring tape on it? On what were its footings sunk; who laid its cornerstone, while the morning stars sang in unison and all the divine beings shouted? Who enclosed

the sea when it burst forth from the womb, when I made the
clouds its garment, the dense clouds its wrap? (Job 38: 4-4)

Humility wasn't the issue. I am well aware that I am not God. And it's not like I felt God owed me this mercy. I wasn't like the elder brother in the parable of the wayward son. (Luke 15:11-32) I didn't feel entitled because I had been "slaving" all of my life for God. I was well aware of my own short comings and didn't see my relationship with God as a quid-pro-quo. The hardest part was that I thought he loved me enough, most important loved Nicole enough, loved my daughter enough, loved our whole family enough, to spare us this unspeakable horror- the death of one we all loved so dearly, the early de-parture of a sweet sweet soul who was so loved here on earth. It was a slap in the face. I told my husband that if I thought he had the ability to spare Nicole and chose not to, I'd never speak to him again. That's how personal it felt. I didn't feel entitled. I just felt abandoned - like I'd been tricked into believing something that just isn't true.

In his book *Disappointment with God* Philip Yancy writes:

One bold message in the book of Job is that you can say anything
to God. Throw at him your grief your anger, your doubt, your
bitterness, your betrayal, your disappointment - he can absorb
them all. As often as not, spiritual giants of the Bible are

shown contending with God. They prefer to go away limping,
like Jacob (Gen. 32:24-26,31) rather than to shut God out.[5]

Lately I've been waking up with a sore arm and hand and now one of my fingers is dislocated, just like Jacob's hip. In my sleep I've been clenching my fist, physically manifesting my distress. It's as though I am shaking my fist towards God, struggling even in my sleep. I am hardly a "spiritual giant" but it's good to know I am in good company in these wrestling matches with God, going away limping. I am out of joint; out of sync with my God.

At Nicole's memorial I said, "I still believe in the goodness of God" and I recounted a story about an anxious couple who was sending their infant son into surgery. The mom turned to the dad and said, "We have to decide right now whether or not God is good, because if we wait to decide that by the results of the surgery, we will always keep God on trial."[6] From where I stand now, that sounds to me like a very easy and very quick assertion.

After God let Nicole die I began to be conscious of previously how often throughout the day I would pray in my head. I'd begin to pray, to ask God for some healing or help or blessing on someone I knew and then I'd abruptly stop when I realized that I no longer trusted this God I had been praying to. If God wouldn't intervene to save the life of a fifteen year old child, why would he bother to be with someone while they took an exam or grant good weather for a wedding? It seemed ludicrous.

I had lost Nicole. But I had also lost in God a good father, a trusted friend, a companion on my life journey. From then on, my longing for Nicole and my longing for God somehow became intertwined.

After watching Nicole endure all of those interventions: the chemo, transfusions, painful physical therapy, the surgeries, and on and on, and then watching her body literally disintegrate before our eyes, how could I not question the whole concept of prayer and who this God really is. Is he The Big Bell Hop in the sky who is there to fulfill our wishes when we ask? Jesus likens him to a stern judge who won't help you unless you are persistent in your pleading. (Luke 18: 1-5) Well that doesn't feel very safe. Yet Jesus more often

> *From then on my longing for Nicole and my longing for God became intertwined.*

portrays God as a loving father. When Jesus was praying in the Garden of Gethsemane at the end of his life he called God "Abba", a term of endearment in Aramaic used for fathers (and one Nicole loved) and of course the Lord's Prayer begins "Our

Father". Jesus calls God "Father" 65 times in the gospels. So for those of us who want to live as Jesus did I guess the best reason to pray is because he did. Still.........Maybe, as the the fourteenth century Persian poet Hafiz says, "God is still hiding in a corner of my heart".

It is said that what you believe about God is the most important thing about you. Theodicy is the conundrum that evil exists in a world created and inhabited by a good and loving God. It seemed I'd have to come to terms with the fact that God is not some kind old grandpa who wants to take the kids out to ice cream.

I was reading recently about an author who was being interviewed about his work. The interviewer asked him if he knew the end of his stories before he wrote them. I'm of a mind that God, like this author, doesn't know the ending of each of our individual stories. That because of free will we are each writing our stories in collaboration with him. I think God knows each of us well enough (just as, if you are parent you know your kids) that he could probably predict what next choice we will make and I think he's cheering us on and hoping we take the right turns. And maybe like a good Father he might just be delighted and even surprised sometimes at how his human creation is navigating the rough waters of life here on Planet Earth. I recently read something that said, "If the door didn't open it wasn't your door." Hmm, well, maybe it WAS "your door" or at least a door that would have taken you to good places, but time and circumstance just didn't allow it. I do believe that in the end love wins - however that may look individually and globally. I believe that God is deeply invested in our particular story and he wants it to be a good one - chapters filled with sound physical, mental, and spiritual health - a life well lived where we each have people to love and people to love us. A story that is a richly layered narrative with beauty and wonderful surprises and astonishments that sometimes take your breath away. A story that anyone would want to read and come away satisfied and maybe even changed.

Father Gregory Boyle, who works with gang intervention in Los Angeles, and is the founder of Homeboy Industries, says in his book *Barking to the Choir,* that his "homies" often talk about two paths. They say that once they were on a bad path and now they are on a good one. But Father Greg says that there really is only one path we humans take. It's a Good Journey that beckons us toward God, a God who loves us and only wants us to be drawn forward toward him. There may be obstacles along the way, grave mistakes made, but this is his intention for us all - one Good Journey.[7] I'm thinking if this good man can remain so seeped in the certainty of God's love after all of the horrors he has witnessed, maybe I can too.

It makes sense that God doesn't change things up down here on earth because he has given us free will and we are not his puppets. He doesn't move us around on some kind of galactic chessboard. Robots are incapable of loving. A love that is programmed is no love at all. If human beings create carcinogens that cause cancer then Nicole and so many others are victims of that. I guess you could say humankind brought this all on ourselves, these painful logical consequences. This is the cost of freedom, this risky frightening freedom. We humans have the freedom to dream, to make beautiful art, to love; or to scheme, destroy, and hate. My journal is full of prayers trying to figure out how God works. Asking, begging him to spare Nicole's life. To intervene. But even after she was gone, I still sought him. At one point I wrote in my journal: *"How about this prayer? God, help me to stop blaming you."* I believe cancer was not God's plan or will for our Nicole.

If I'm more confused about who God is, I think I am that much more certain about who Jesus is and was when he walked the earth. Earlier I said I felt I had lost "a good father, a trusted friend, a companion on my life journey". Unconsciously I had named the three persons of the trinity! Father, Son, and Holy Spirit. This is true: I love and believe in a Jesus who wept and healed and loved tenderly. And I believe in a Spirit who, when we simply don't know how to pray, *"intercedes for us with sighs too deep for words"*. (Romans 8:26) Of all of the thousands of words written in the Bible, I think that phrase is one of the most beautiful. It's so personal, so down deep. I am hanging on to it by a thread.

I am reminded of a scene described in the book of John. It was a time when many of Jesus's followers were turning away from him, because Jesus had a radical way of stirring things up- asking people to open their minds to his new teachings about so many things. So Jesus asked the twelve, "Do you also want to leave?" And the disciple Peter replied, "To whom would we go? You have the words of real life, eternal life." (John 6:67-68 The Message) I am far from an expert or learned scholar on the world's religions. But I have studied enough to know that Jesus is where my heart is. I always come home to him. And that will have to be enough. Yes indeed, where else would I go? His are the words that have eternal truths for me, valid for all time.

More and more I am finding a home in this kind of contemplative prayer that depends on the Spirit to intercede for me. I am trying to trust God with my war-torn heart, seeking a God that is both beyond me and yet within me. Luke 5:15 tells us that "Jesus often withdrew to lonely places and prayed." I have to say I love this contemplative side of Jesus. A man who sought prayerful solace up on a mountainside (Matthew 14:23) and by the sea (Matthew 14:13) and in a garden (Mark

14:32). I feel a kinship, a closeness, to this God/man because I find solace and reassurance in these places too.

"Prayer is then not just a formula of words, or a series of desires springing up in the heart - it is the orientation our whole body, mind, and spirit to God in silence, attention and adoration. All good meditative prayer is a conversation of our entire self to God," says Thomas Merton.

And Saint Basil: *"This is how you pray continually - not by offering prayer in words, but by joining yourself to God through your whole way of life, so that your life becomes one continuous and uninterrupted prayer."*

This is exactly what Nicole's Good Friday prayer was that I wrote about earlier. It was a true communion with God. We cheapen and trivialize prayer if we think it's only about asking for what we want. Contemplative prayer is more about the inner journey of opening ourselves up to what God has for us in the moment. And the good news is we can trust that when we simply don't have the words, the Spirit will intercede for us. Psalm 42: 7 says: *"Deep calls to deep in the roar of your waterfalls."*

The Psalms in the Bible were Jesus's prayer book. As a Jewish boy growing up in Nazareth, he would have memorized many of these ancient poems. The Psalms of Lament are expressions of heart break and feelings of abandonment but the psalmist always also includes vows of trust and praise. These ancient vows of trust and praise are ways of remembering the times when God was near and faithful - a lifeline to one whose heart is shattered. My heart is with the psalmist in Psalm 143 - a psalm of lament -when he says:

> *My spirit grows faint within me; my heart within me is dismayed. I remember the days of long ago. I meditate on all your works and consider what your hands have done.*

During these hard times I am making an effort to remember, as this Psalm says, what he has done.

Anne Lamott has famously said, "Faith is hope with a track record". If I'm honest of course there is evidence that God has a good "track record" in my life. There must have been thousands of times God's angels protected those I love and me from harm. I believe this. I feel His presence with me often, nudging me along in the right direction if I pay attention.

The ancient Israelites erected ebenezers, stone monuments, to remind themselves what God had done for them. I have many of these stones of hope in my life and to survive this devastating hurricane I found myself caught up in, I began to draw little stacks of stones in my journal and notes to remind myself of the times that God has been on this journey with me. I was trying to rediscover God. Trying to reassure myself that he was still the good father I had counted on.

I was raised by a single mom in the 1950's and it was often a hard life for my family. Born in St. Joseph's Hospital in a small town in the midwest, my mom told me that the nuns baptized me there and I have always intuited that whatever blessings they said over me stuck. I was blessed to be able to attend Immanuel Lutheran elementary school in that same town where I was born. The word Immanuel means "God with us". And he was. Those eight years were certainly foundational to my faith. I have had wonderful, kind, smart, nurturing people in my path who have guided me and loved me throughout my life. How could love like that not come from God himself?

I know that keeping a soft heart is imperative for my mental health and spiritual growth.

Anne Lamott, in her book *Stitches*, says:

> *The good news is that if you don't seal up your heart with caulking compound, and instead stay permeable, people stay alive inside you, and maybe outside you too, forever.*[8]

If keeping an open heart, no matter how painful, will help me keep Nicole in some way then I will do that. Gladly.

Growing up, when things went wrong my default emotion was often anger. It was a smoke screen for the true emotion of sadness, easier to get mad rather than acknowledge any heartache. When Nicole was taken from us I was afraid to go there. I didn't want to get angry at God because it felt like a dark road to a dark place from which I might not return. It's been said that if you scratch a cynic, just underneath the skin is a hopeful romantic, someone protecting a tender heart because they want so much to believe in some goodness in this world. I think that is true of me. I knew I needed to remember those ebenezers, and remember that we, as Christians, are Easter people with hope just on the other side of grief.

The bottom line is I believe God created Nicole and that he loved her. There is no answer to the WHY he let her suffer and die. He did not spare even his only son from an early painful death or the disciples who were martyred. God is omnipotent, omnipresent- powerful and everywhere. But there is still a little voice within me that says I don't need a God who is everywhere. I need a God to be here. With me.

To state the obvious, there's a lot of suffering in this world. We were and are certainly not the only ones who have faced tribulation: people in war-torn countries, those in refugee camps, abused children, and on and on. My friend told me something her husband who died of cancer said when talking about his diagnosis: "Not why me? But why *not* me?" I don't think I've ever heard a more generous thought from a human being. I will never be able to say "Well, why not Nicole?" because she was a child. Our child. And the desire to protect her was enormous. For a while in my darkest days I began to despair that maybe our family was somehow cursed. But then I would remember that our family, uniquely, was a million times more blessed just to have had Nicole in our lives. *We* were the ones who got to have her among us- this girl with her intelligence, her big heart and big wit and her playful spirit.

Sometimes this breath prayer helps:

breathe in: God be in my heart
breathe out: Take away my hunger for answers

Chapter Eleven

She's Got a Way About Her

A

nne Lamott writes:

> *When my friend Pammy was dying at the age of 37, her doctor told me, "Watch her carefully now because she's teaching us how to live."*[9]

Oh how profound. And how true this was of Nicole. Despite everything, despite the fact that she knew her days were now limited, she had many good days with friends and family. After they discontinued the chemo and she had been off it for three months her hair came back in a cute curly pixie cut. And her mom gave her the okay for a tiny nose pierce that held a sparkly gem on the left side of her nostril. She looked darling and her whole face emanated light.

> *When my friend Pammy was dying at the age of 37, her doctor told me, "Watch her carefully now, because she's teaching us how to live."*

Once Nicole and I went to one of those shops where you paint and fire your own pottery. I chose a small votive that had a heart cut out where the light from the candle could shine out. It sits on my bookshelf now and reminds me of how the fire of Nicole's suffering must have refined her - burned away all of the bad stuff that the rest of us carry around. Her light shone. And it was evident in her face, her smile, and in her just plain goodness.

That Thanksgiving was our last time together as a family. We celebrated at Nana Trish and Papa Dan's home and enjoyed Nana's usual outstanding culinary skills. With a fire in the fireplace and football on the t.v. it seemed as normal as it could be under the circumstances. The four West Coast cousins had their usual sweet time together and when Papa Dan took them out for a spin in his golf cart Nicole kept him laughing, was her usual witty self, making jokes and teasing.

That fall MacKenzie rented a house near Yosemite and invited all of Nicole's friends, fourteen in all, to spend a few days of fun. A caravan of cars full of rafts, blow up beds, matching pajama bottoms, and enough food for an army made its way to the lake. There was much frivolity and joy and the kids were compassionate and loving when Nicole had to take long naps in between being in the healing waters of the lake and enjoying all the revelry. These were true friends, sticking by her at her weakest most vulnerable time. A gift. What would it be like to lose a treasured friend at such an impressionable age?

Right before Jesus was seized for crucifixion, when He knew He wouldn't be on this earth much longer, he said to his friends:

I give you a new commandment: Love each other. Just as I

have loved you, so you must also love each other. This is how everyone will know that you are my disciples, when you love each other. (John 13:33-34)

Of all of the things Jesus could have advised his people to do, loving each other was the most important. He could have advised them: Organize, form an army against the Romans, build some more temples, construct some beautiful cities, set up some monuments. But no. He simply said, "Love one another".

Nicole was only fifteen when she left this planet. She hadn't earned a PhD, become the CEO of her own company, won a Nobel Peace Prize; she hadn't even had time to add a high school diploma to her resume. But Nicole knew how to love. She had that down pat.

Nicole was indeed teaching us how to live. Over and over again when people describe Nicole they note how unselfish, how loving, how full of joy she was. She would light up every room she entered. Our friend Michelle, when describing Nicole, said that Nicole had the unique ability to make every person feel so loved and so special. It was authentic. I know she really did see each person as a child of God. When Nicole greeted Michelle she would often exclaim, "THERE you are!" As though she'd been waiting to be with her, had been missing her so much.

One of Nicole's main concerns that she shared with me and with others was that her mom and Natalie would be taken care of. At fifteen, she was taking over the role of matriarch of her little family.

Chapter Twelve

Blue Hawaii

Hawaii vacations have always provided a place of fun, love, warmth, and togetherness for our family. Wanting to capture this feeling one last time, we planned a trip for the first part of December. It was a disaster. Even traumatizing. Nicole knew the trip was for her and would be her last and it sent a very bad vibe over the whole time. I cannot imagine what was happening in her sweet and tender fifteen year old heart and soul but I know she did not want to accept that she was going to die. Suddenly she was failing fast, in pain, and on a lot of medications that made her woozy and clumsy and nauseous. She wasn't comfortable in the ocean that she usually loved so much, and was only marginally able to laugh and have fun with her cousins. She was spending a lot of time in bed in the condo talking on the phone with her friends. We didn't know it yet but the tumor was pressing on her spine by then and it was making her legs unsteady. Trying to brighten the time, I took her shopping for gifts that she wanted to take home to her friends. In the store she dropped several breakable items and when they shattered to the floor I felt frantic and out of control. Finally I got her outdoors just in time for her to vomit into a trashcan.

She was in a lot of pain. And on the plane on the way home as she was walking down the aisle with her mom behind her she lost complete control of her legs and had to grasp onto the seats on either side of her to steady herself. I was already in my seat across the aisle from where she would sit and I watched in horror. It was a scene I will never be able to erase from my mind. I turned my face to the window and wept bitter hot tears. I didn't want her to see me. But of course she was aware of her Mimi and once in the air, after her mom got her settled and gallantly wrestled compression hosiery onto her feet and legs, Nicole looked over at me with compassion and sadness in her eyes and passed me a note that she had scribbled on a scrap of paper. I am full of deep regret that I lost track of it along the way but I remember it said that I should reach out to my Abba and that he was Love. Classic Nicole giving love and comfort when she was the one who needed it most.

Chapter Thirteen

Homecoming

MacKenzie had made the decision to transfer Nicole's care to Lucile Packard Children's Hospital at Stanford. Not because the care wasn't quality where she had been, but because she felt more comfortable with the pediatric oncologist there who was more personable and seemed much more eager to try different strategies to provide comfort for Nicole as we tried to navigate these days.

Nicole was admitted off and on, took many trips to the ER, and endured so many procedures, until it was finally decided on December 16 to bring her home and Hospice would come in and provide needed care. I sent a three word text out to my friends: "Hospice is in." Three devastating words that said it all. We were on the home stretch.

At the hospital we were discussing how Nicole would be transported home because she wasn't able to sit up and ride in a car. When we told her an ambulance would bring her home I cautioned her that she shouldn't worry or be alarmed because they wouldn't have the red lights flashing. Typically, Nicole replied, "Well they better!" She wanted to make a grand departure and a grand entrance home. It was almost midnight by the time the ambulance arrived so once again Nicole was making a night journey home from the hospital. But this time without me and without any singing. And this journey would be her last. Of course she chatted with the young cute EMT all the way home. I can only imagine what he must have thought. Here was this beautiful teenaged girl, dying, but so full of good spirits and humor.

The next day I wrote in my journal:

> *It was a strangely joyous homecoming last night. Relieved to have her home in her nest. No more painful IV's, no one poking and prodding our girl. Just love and light and warmth and a cheery light-filled nook off the kitchen with a garden view - cooking and friends and soon an in-home pedicure from her Mimi. <u>Her light still shines.</u>*

Now I had only one desperate prayer left: *God, please deliver her peacefully into the arms of Jesus.*

Chapter Fourteen

Homegoing

In our geographic area the Hospice care for children is called Kidwise. In our case the team was made up of two nurses, Ally and Rhio, and one doctor, Dr. Walker. Each made us feel like we were the only family on earth. We had their full love and attention. They were present without being intrusive and their quiet strength and compassion was so needed as Nicole made her pilgrimage home.

Nicole made a special connection with each of them, but Rhio was the one who noticed the tattoo on Nicole's ankle and they made a deal that Rhio would get one too.

The days wore on, Nicole tucked into her small hospital bed in the dining area of her home. Her mom, Auntie Courtney, and I puttered around the kitchen, making cookies that no one really wanted to eat.

As Nicole began to seem farther and farther away from us a musical theme emerged. We knew that even if she couldn't interact with us, music would be a balm for her. Once a retired pastor friend, Brad, came and many of MacKenzie's friends gathered around Nicole's bed and Brad anointed Nicole and we all prayed and sang. On an especially spirit filled evening Nicole's friends Kennan and Savannah came and played their guitars and the whole house was filled with deep love and the sound of Nicole's friends singing. It was overwhelming.

Finally, on December 27, 2023 a quietness settled over the house. Things just felt different. The Celtics call this a "thin place". A mysterious feeling that somehow God is near and the space between heaven and earth is thin. MacKenzie, Courtney, and I all spent time sitting with Nicole, holding her hand, each telling her how much we loved her. I sang soft lullabies to her and when her Poppa came over he sat by her bed and played songs from his phone that he and she had previously shared a love for.

Thirteen year old Natalie asked for some privacy and she went and stretched herself out on the bed next to her sister and whispered words of love and gratitude that she was able to be her sister. Mack gave her permission to go over to a close friend's home and then it was just Mack, Courtney, and me in the house.

Nurse Rhio had come in the morning and after telling us she thought Nicole's passing was eminent, she reminded us that a couple of weeks earlier before Nicole began slipping away and was still lucid she had made a date with me to come to my house, pick up some burgers from the local joint, and have a Bible study, just the two of us, and then a sleepover. Nicole named the date: December 27th - and her mom and Rhio and I made eye contact over her head and shared a silent wink. We all knew that Nicole was not going to emerge from that bed.

But I heartedly assured Nicole that it was a date! Yes, we would definitely be having that special time on that particular day.

By 2:30 on that day, Nicole's mom, her Auntie Courtney and I all felt the urge to be especially close by our girl. Nicole couldn't focus or speak - so much like a newborn baby. We gazed and gazed into her face, telling her how much we loved her, stroking her face softly and murmuring to her as you would a baby new to this world. We watched for any little turn of her lips, any smile or recognition in her face. She was not new to this world, but she was going to be new to another. She was making her final exit here on earth and it felt dreamlike. A mix of emotions and vibrations swirled around her bed that were most certainly not of this world. They say the dying process is a lot like the birth process and this was evident now. Now we sensed that she was living between two realities, two worlds. One world that we three knew nothing about. In a little while it seemed there was a lot of energy surrounding the bed and we three began to quietly cheer her on. Each of softly speaking at once. *It's okay to go little girl. You can fly away now. Jesus is waiting for you. No more pain. Run free!*

At last, Nicole drew her final breath and her heart stopped. She had gone on to glory. Courtney looked at the clock and she said, "It's 3:30."

❧

Mack hurried over to the the friend's house where Natalie was visiting to tell her the news. When Lila, the mom, opened the door and saw Mack standing there she said, "Nicole is gone." And Mack said yes. Lila replied that at around 3:15 she got very still and felt chills go down her spine. She knew that Nicole was there. I believe that Nic had come to tell her little sister goodbye one last time.

❧

I headed home that night, picked up some burgers and settled in the bunk room where all the grandkids have spent so many overnights at our house. I opened the Bible to Psalm 139 and through tears, read it aloud. (see Appendix B)

❧

The next day I was sitting in my little den/library that is right off the bunk room and my eyes caught the sight of a little clock I have sitting on the bookshelf. It was stopped at 3:15. Maybe she was early for our date, or had come to tell her Poppa goodbye. Either way, it seems her little spirit had been making the rounds.

Chapter Fifteen

Awe

S ole Sisters is a hiking group inspired and created by my friend Darci. Over many years I have been on hiking and camping trips with this group in various places in California - from Big Sur, along the central coast, up to San Francisco and Marin county, and over to Yosemite- moving through majestic redwood groves, walking over ancient stones, breathing the salt air of the magnificent Pacific Ocean, feeling the spray of stunning waterfalls. On these treks I am reminded that you cannot be in a state of awe and feel bereft at the same time. You cannot hold a sense of wonder and sadness all at once. "It will be solved in the walking," said Saint Augustine. And I have found this to be true. If not *solved* then *resolved,* bringing me back to some state of harmony. The miraculous enormity of nature reminds me of just how small I am. There have been times when, sitting in the house at night, I just had to get out from under the roof of our home and go outdoors and look up. Look up at the stars and feel the vastness of the universe and confirm that there is some life force out there that I cannot understand.

On hikes, as I have taken one step at a time in these places of wonder, through every season I've felt in my bones an assurance that life in the cosmos would go on, was currently going on as it had been since the beginning of time. And so would Nicole go on too. Shouldn't I be able to trust a God who created all of this beauty, this web of life where every organism depends upon another? There must be a rhyme and reason here to be trusted.

Theologian and writer Philip Yancy tells a story about hiking in Colorado with a friend. When the friend tells him that there is a foxes' den nearby Philip wonders if they will see the foxes that day. The friend replies that he doesn't know - he says they are wild animals you know, and they do what they please. That is sometimes how I see God. Of course there is the familiar metaphor of God as Aslan the lion in *The Lion, The Witch and the Wardrobe.* But in that depiction of God he is said to be good but not safe. This animal God that I am drawn to feels like a different kind of wild God to me. A holy wild and free God who lives among beauty and who is part of that beauty. Enmeshed in that beauty. I can almost smell the musky smell he would emit. Wild. Mysterious. Untamable.

When Nicole was little I took her to Big Basin State Park and we walked amidst the redwoods and I passed a lesson on to her that Darci had passed on to the Sole Sisters about the wisdom of the redwood trees. I told Nicole that our family is like a redwood grove. We are each dependent upon each other for nourishment, strength and stability. Redwood trees have shallow roots and would soon collapse if not for the stabilizing roots of other trees in its circle. The little sprouts that grow around the circle make up what are called fairy rings and the trees use the nutrients and root systems of the more mature trees in order to flourish. When a parent tree dies this new generation of trees rises and the root systems of old trees continue to grow for a time and nourish the younger trees even after they die. All of this is a steady process since redwoods can grow up to 350 feet tall and can live for thousands of years. Life is slow and steady in the forest. There is a comforting predictability to it. Life and death. The dead fallen leaves now black from the rain serve as rich compost for new life. Death and resurrection. I think that day Nicole felt the soul deep interconnectedness of our family and our place in the grandeur of nature.

The book of Genesis tells a story about a God who is the ultimate gardener, artist, and designer. In the account in Genesis God uses the Hebrew word Adamah (Adam) to describe the first human being. Adamah translates as earth, soil, dirt, or humus.

> *Then God said, "Let us make man in our image, in our likeness, and let <u>them</u> rule over the fish of the sea and the birds of the air, over the livestock, over all the earth, and over all the creatures that move along the ground. So God created man in his own image, in the image of God he created him; male and female he created them. ....The Lord God had not sent rain on the earth and there was no man to work the*

ground but streams came up from the earth and watered the whole surface of the ground - the Lord God formed the man from the dust of the ground and breathed into his nostrils the breath of life and man became a living being. (Genesis 1: 26, 27 and Genesis 2:57)

Formed from the dust of the ground and saturated with streams that came up and watered the whole surface of the earth, his mud babies were now to be stewards of this good place he had created and gifted them. Human beings were to have dominion - not domination- over the natural world. Wonder. Awe.

Chapter Sixteen

Across the Universe

T he spacecraft was billions of miles away and the image of Planet Earth looked just like a fuzzy dot amid a streak of sunlight. Gazing at this image, Carl Sagan remarked,

> *Look at that dot. There's here. That's home. That's us. On it everyone you love, everyone you know, everyone you ever heard of, every human being who ever was lived out their lives. The aggregate of our joy and suffering, thousands of confident relations, ideologies and economic doctrines, every hunter and forager, hero and coward, every creator and destroyer of civilization, every king and every peasant, every young couple in love, every mother and father, hopeful child, inventor and explorer, every teacher of morals, every corrupt politician, every 'superstar' and 'supreme leader', every saint and sinner in the history of our species lived there - on a mote of dust suspended in a sunbeam.[10]*

The Message is a modern translation of the Bible written by Eugene Peterson. In the introduction to the book of Matthew, the first book of the gospels, Peterson writes:

> *The story of Jesus doesn't begin with Jesus. God had been at work for a long time…. Every day we wake up in the middle of something that is already going on, something that has been going on for a long time: genealogy and geology, history and culture, the cosmos - God.[11]*

I just love this so much and find such comfort in these words. It makes me know that I don't see the whole picture . I see only just one tiny microsecond in God's unfathomable universe. The awful pain and loss of my Nicole is just one part of the story. What is monumentally huge to me can only be put into perspective by trusting that there is a loving God out there. Or better yet - here with us. I am trying to believe this is true. I want to believe in this God that is too big for us to imagine in our finite minds.

Here is God described by Mark Buchanan in his book *Your God is Too Safe:*

> *Nietzsche was wrong. We haven't killed God, we just domesticated Him. We've made Him too safe, too soft, too fastidious. In our moments of sentimentality, we allow the He might dwell in hushed cathedrals, musty cloisters, tranquil forests, the laughter of children, the soft petals of roses, blah blah blah. But not, surely, not in the jostling, brawling world of our doings and undoings.. In boardrooms and bedchambers, in lecture halls and marketplaces.* [12]

This is the God I want to imagine and hold in my heart. A God who is everywhere. In my best moments I feel like, yes, there is something huge and beautiful and trustworthy going on around me that I cannot see or understand. That the loss of precious Nicole is only a minute piece of some larger magnificent puzzle. And all will be revealed one day. All in good time.

Chapter Seventeen

Water

W ater is life-giving. It's the stuff we are made of. As I write this I am aware that while we in this country enjoy our swimming pools and hot tubs, bathtubs and sinks filled to the brim, while we stand under shower heads for long periods of time and let this precious commodity beat down on our heads, much of the rest of the world is literally dying for lack of it. Depending on the source you read, it is said that in the Bible water is mentioned between 500 and 2,000 times. It is a symbol for the renewing and sustaining love of God.

In his book *Everything Belongs* Richard Rohr tell us, "Don't push the river." He says God's love is like a flowing river and we are flowing with it, in it. We don't need to push it. We can trust that we don't need to manufacture easy answers to hard questions if we trust the continuous providential care God has for us. Without this awareness we succumb to fear and wanting to take control.[13]

After we lost Nicole I developed a deep desire to be a part of this flow. I wanted so much to relax into a belief in God's goodness and his love for our family, but I was a woman on the shore with the smell and taste of the ocean in my face, struggling to launch her kayak, seeing the vast ocean (which is now made up of rivers' flow) out there where the currents were moving along -but struggling- unable to get over the waves in order to get into this continuous rhythmic life force.

Water has been an on-going theme in my life. At age sixty I learned to swim partly inspired by four year old Nicole who loved the water right from the beginning. When my daughters were small I lived vicariously through them, watching them excel on a swim team. When Nicole was born her Auntie Courtney and I cupped her long little feet in our hands and looked at each other. *Yep, we said. Swimmer's feet.* To my delight, Nicole carried on this legacy and earned many ribbons on a swim team too. I loved taking her to meets - standing with the long aqua blue lanes stretched out before me, taking in the faint whiff of chlorine and imagining myself back in the days when my girls had swum in meets too. Little Nicole would burst off the starting block and a competitive spirit that I didn't know was there would take over. Her little arms would be chopping staccato like through the clear blue water until she reached the end of the lane and her little face would emerge with a look of triumph and pride when she realized she'd come in first.

Until I gathered up all of my courage and took a series of swimming lessons, my childhood fear of water left me sitting in the boat or on the shore as the rest of the family snorkeled and swam on our vacations to Hawaii. In the years that followed, now I could join all of my grandchildren, these little mermaids and mermen, in the water.

When Nicole was stuck in the hospital during chemo and after she became too weak and sick to be up and around, I would bring her seashells from my morning walks on the beach. I would press the shell into her hand and ask her to bring it to her face and take in the healing smell of the ocean and even taste the salt on the surface of this beautiful gift from the sea.

With my new found skill, lap swimming in the salt water pool at my athletic club has become a saving grace for me. I shared earlier that Nicole and I were unable to weep together after we found out the cancer had metastasized to her spine. Just a few weeks after Nicole had passed I was swimming laps, listening to music on my waterproof earbuds. The song "Even If" by MercyMe came on whose lyrics are based on some words in the book of Daniel 3:16-18. In this scripture three young men: Shadrach, Meshach, and Abednego have been ordered by King Nebuchadnezzar to enter a blazing furnace because they will not denounce the God of the Hebrews. They boldly assert that the God they serve will deliver them from this death, but then they say that EVEN IF HE DOESN'T they will still honor their God. Whew. Well, in our case, in Nicole's case, God DIDN'T. And my heart burst open as the full reality of that hit me. I was suddenly enveloped in the salt water of the pool on my skin and the salt water going down my throat and the salt water of my tears that were filling up my goggles. I made it to the side of the pool and turned my face to the concrete and wept and wept like I have never wept before. I was completely overcome with grief, overcome and surrounded by this water that refused to buoy me. In that moment I distinctly felt Nicole's presence and I know as surely as I know anything that she was weeping with me. I know many will say that people don't weep in heaven but here was our chance, Nicole's and my chance, to finally break down and weep together and let out all of the sorrow we said we couldn't release that day we talked at breakfast. The tears we said we couldn't share had finally come.

Chapter Eighteen

The Ravens

For many years now I have been working as a volunteer ranch hand at a facility that used to serve those with physical disabilities. I tend to a herd of donkeys, mucking up after them and grooming them and caring for them. Because donkeys are such affectionate, solid, dependable animals, these ancient animals had served as therapy donkeys for the people who came for help. Science tells us that when we are around animals our heart and breathing rates slow, our blood pressure drops, and our muscles relax. Tapping into an animal's energy field can be a balm for your soul. Each week, all alone in the quiet, I can hear only the sound of my own breath and an occasional bray of a donkey. Working steadily out under the redwoods, soaking up the good earth and spending time with God's good creatures, I am at perfect peace. I feel a kind of reverence and gratitude that makes time stands still.

One morning when I arrived at work I was met by the sound of ravens cawing. Looking up into the sky, I saw dozens of ravens circling in the air all around the ranch. It looked almost like they had been choreographed into a dance. It seemed pretty obvious that there was some kind of ritual going on. This went on for days. The owner of the property, Lori, and I discussed it and I went home and through some reading discovered that these beautiful shiny black birds with their great hooked beaks were performing a funeral ritual![14] I came back the next day and told Lori what I had read and she looked at me with wide eyes. She had found the body of a raven in a planter box. We surmised that this was the body of a raven that had been given to the ranch as a baby - a rescued fledgling-twenty years ago. I would often see this guy and his mate in the mornings. Lori would throw bread on the roof of the house and he and his partner would come and share it. If Lori left a special treat like an egg on the bench below, he would come down and eat some and then take some to his partner who waited for him on the roof. I believe that these birds doing this beautiful dance in the sky were

> *Animals behave in ways that astonish us if we just pay attention. I guess God is like that too.*

probably his offspring and through the wonder of nature it had been communicated to them that the grandaddy of them all had died and they had all come to pay their respects. And maybe, like humans, to sort out who would now assume the patriarchal role. Either way, here was a community of creatures coming together in much the same way we do when a loved one is lost to us.

Animals behave in ways that astonish us if we just pay attention. I guess God is like that too.

Chapter Nineteen

The Soundtrack of
Her Life

Human beings have rich and beautiful traditional ways to remember and honor their dead. From sitting shiva, to second line parades in New Orleans, to wakes, to celebrations during Dia de los Muertos, to somber funeral services, they all have one thing in common: community. It is the presence of loved ones who comfort the family and close friends of the one who is no longer there that make life bearable to those who are the survivors.

Never was this more evident than in the way the whole community showed up in so many ways for MacKenzie and Natalie. In a situation of terrible and awkward timing, the townhouse that Mack had been trying for months to buy suddenly was a reality. With all of the hospital stays and numerous trips to doctors' offices, MacKenzie was totally unprepared to make this move. And she needed to move quickly. MacKenzie is a school counselor in her little town and she is known and loved by many. I will never forget the way scores of moms and dads showed up at her apartment and literally packed her up and carried her belongings to her new place. Her four closest friends on the school staff had spent hours organizing, sorting, putting things in boxes. When I showed up at her new place, there were dads sitting on the floor putting together dressers and bookshelves and moms in the kitchen organizing spices, dishes, pots and pans. It was overwhelming. When MacKenzie and Nicole arrived home from Stanford Children's Hospital late one night that December, there in the living room was a sparkling Christmas tree illuminating the whole house with warmth and love.

The morning of January 21, 2024 dawned like any other winter morning on the central coast of California. Nicole's memorial service was to take place in a beautiful chapel at the base of the Santa Cruz mountains and I was worried that the rain that was so common this time of year would make it too difficult for people to navigate the roads and find parking places among the redwoods' fallen needles. As the day wore on there was no rain. But I had other things to worry about. I was just consumed with anxiety. It wasn't stage fright because I was one of the speakers. I was focused on honoring Nicole and there were a lot of things I needed to say. It was because this just seemed so final, such a last goodbye. I couldn't bear it. I couldn't eat and by the time I left for the service at dusk my stomach was roiling and burning and my legs were unsteady.

When I entered the chapel, however, things changed in an instant. There was the band that was comprised of Nicole's friends up on stage warming up, the acoustics sending chills down my spine, filling every cell in my body. There were MacKenzie's closest and dearest friends bustling around, preparing this sacred space, busy filling the chapel with the most beautiful flowers I've ever seen. I learned later that MacKenzie's friend,

Sarah, had taken flowers and greenery from the elementary, middle and high schools that Nicole had attended and had incorporated them into the bouquets. But best of all, there on the screen at the front of the sanctuary, high above, was a large photo of my girl, Nicole, smiling down on all of us. The words of Jesus Christ were scripted underneath:

> *In the same way, let your light shine before others, that they may see your good deeds and glorify your Father in heaven. (Matthew 5:16)*

Knowing that MacKenzie was experiencing some of my same symptoms, I quickly grabbed my phone and wrote out a text to her: *God is here; Nicole is here; it's all going to be all right.* I hit "send" hoping this short missive would give her strength for the day.

A few months earlier Nicole's surfing teacher had also succumbed to cancer. Nicole attended his celebration of life and she told me that he had wanted to think of his dying as a "graduation". And I believe this was Nicole's wish too. Here among all those who loved her and loved our family was the celebration of her commencement into a different, holy space.

As the service began, it was standing room only and as the band began to play, all 500 of us got to our feet and began to sing with the girl we all came to honor looking down on us and smiling. I could hardly contain the love and joy that filled every part of me. There was my husband sitting solidly, as usual, beside me; there were my remaining grandchildren and their parents tucked in all around me. The room was on fire with the Spirit. In that moment, God and Nicole were as alive to me as every person in that sanctuary.

> *The room was on fire with the Spirit. In that moment, God and Nicole were as alive to me as every person in that sanctuary.*

After Nicole left us and her mom was going through her phone she found a playlist entitled: "Plan B". The child had subtly, secretly planned out the music for her memorial. So these were the songs we heard.

Among them was a song I would often play as I cooked while Nicole sat at the kitchen table chatting with me. It was "You and I Again" by James Taylor. The song talks about regrets that time cannot be slowed and the wish to recapture lost moments. Once as I was humming along to this tune, Nicole asked me what I would think of when I listened to that song. I stupidly said I guessed I would think of the love I have for her Poppa. Now I know that one phrase about wishing to slow things down must have been so meaningful and mournful for her. I don't think I'll ever be able to listen to that song again.

I wish I'd caught it and asked her to talk more about what *she* was thinking. These days, I often write Nicole little chatty notes in my journal and they are always accompanied by a line drawing of two women with the caption "You and I Again".

Several of Nicole's friends spoke. A striking juxtaposed visual- these lovely young teenagers with their bright beautiful faces standing at the doorway to the rest of their lives speaking at a funeral. I think every one of them said they were Nicole's best friend because Nicole was able to make these heart and soul connections with each of her friends. Even before she got sick she didn't have a lot time for surface relationships.

One friend, Julia, noted that she and Nicole had a strong bond around music. One of their favorite songs was "Vienna" by Billy Joel which was also on Nicole's "Plan B" list and was played at the memorial. Julia said she and Nicole especially liked the lyrics because they talk about slowing down and not trying to accomplish everything all at once.

There it was again, that awareness of time. And Nicole knew she was running out of it. But now Nicole is living outside of time, wherever that may be. However that may look. Another mystery. Something our human minds cannot comprehend. Another call to trust.

As we gathered in the woodsy reception hall after the service, everyone had big smiles on their faces and there were so many embraces, so many friends, so much warmth. Among literally hundreds of others, I was so touched to see the staff of Kidwise. And of course there was Rhio, who lifted up her pant leg to show us a tiny heart tattoo on her ankle.

Chapter Twenty

Grief in the Kingdom of God

Instead of "I miss you" the French translation is "You are missing from me." How true this is for me. I think, for me, there are only two stages of grief: the person I was when Nicole was here and the person I am now. If grief is the price you pay for love then all of us who knew Nicole are paying dearly. Our family as a whole and the individual lives of those in our family would not have been the same without her and they are not the same now.

I admit there have been times when I feel afraid to move on, wanting to keep a part of me in this sadness, thinking that if I stop this grieving I'll lose her altogether. She'll float away like some sprite- I'm thinking that if my sorrow leaves, she'll leave too. I want to keep her real beside me where, even if I cannot see her or touch her, I can still feel her presence. Not long after Nicole left us MacKenzie and I took an art class that was taught by a woman who had been Nicole's fifth grade teacher, someone she loved and admired. During the class I'd conjure Nicole up - visualize her sitting in one of the folding chairs, relaxing with her beautiful long legs crossed (the scar was still there) one elbow relaxing over the back of the chair. There she was with her sweet little pixie haircut and mischievous smile, head thrown back, laughing and making funny comments.

One of the things I was able to say to Nicole when we knew her time was limited is this: "Nic, I'm 72 years old. And I'm right behind you." I know time is different in God's kingdom and I am so happy that I expressed to her many times that our love is eternal. Scripture says:

> *But do not overlook this one fact, beloved, that with the Lord one day is as a thousand years, and a thousand years as one day. (2 Peter 3:8)*

One day, paging through my journal, I noticed that on September 3, 2022 just twelve days before Nicole was first diagnosed, I recounted a dream I had had the night before. It was one of those dreams that seems more like a vision because the colors are so bright, so vivid. I dreamed I was holding a frog in my hand. It was the brightest emerald green and half of its body was covered with sparkling jewels of many colors. In the dream I showed it to MacKenzie and handed it to her. It is said that frogs symbolize rebirth but of course then I didn't know we were about to witness a monumental transformation in Nicole. What was God trying to tell me? Maybe that even if this transformation was going to be hard and ugly there will be ultimate beauty? I don't know. It will take some time for this to be a salve for my grief. They say grief itself can be transformational......this is a process that I am quietly mindful of.

This deep grief is a new experience for me. Sometimes it's

like a razor cut that is deep and exquisite. Sometimes it's an expansion in my gut and in my chest and a deep aliveness comes over me. All of my senses are on high alert. It is something more real that I've ever felt and it tells me I am human. It tells me that I'm a part of the dust that makes up all of us. I am a human being- one of God's own mud babies - who has been given the capacity to love deeply- and with loving deeply comes suffering deeply- the intensity of my grief mirroring the love I had for Nic.

I believe that if people don't allow themselves to feel pain, they won't feel joy either. And just because I'm struggling doesn't mean I'm failing. I sometimes think the Middle Eastern cultures have it right - keening and wailing at the loss of one they loved so deeply. I must accept that what was will never be again. Our family has been irreparably changed. For whoever else we are - individually and collectively- we are the family who has lost one of its children. This is part of who we are now. I cannot be fully alive if I do not recognize this sorrow, this loneliness, this feeling of betrayal. The first century bishop Irenaeus said, "Woman fully alive is the glory of God." (well, he actually said "man", but....) God created the whole package, not just one dimensional puppets who parrot trite well-worn phrases: "Everything happens for a reason" "God must have needed another angel in heaven", or the absolute worst, "God doesn't give you more than you can handle" which is completely non-Biblical and out of context. The temptation might be to just skip right over the pain and go straight to scriptures that provide temporary relief without really absorbing the scripture's context, intention, or meaning. I don't need to twist myself up in a theological pretzel to try and figure out the why of it. Or just keep myself so busy I cannot slow down and just feel. I have accepted that I am in a kind of grief recovery. It's one day at a time. I must tend to my heart now each day, being honest, and intentionally keeping my heart soft and open. This soul work will never be done. Bluntly put, I need to own up to where I really am on this journey because if I'm faking it, then it makes God fake too.

I've learned that if you do not consciously acknowledge the depth of your grief, your body will do it for you. Trauma can be stored in the body and have serious ramifications later on.

In her book, *The Grieving Body*, Mary Frances O'Connor explains this mind/body/spirit/connection to grief. She writes:

> *When a loved one dies it's not just our brain that responds. Our reaction to loss is not only in our thoughts our emotions, our mind. The response to the death of a loved one is a physiological one as well, reverberating throughout our body. Bereaved people show increased heart rate, blood pressure, stress hormones, inflammation.....when 'you' and 'me' turn into 'us' through*

bonding, and then the 'us' has a piece cut away...when this
amputation happens, we do not return to the 'me' before....[15]

Just acknowledging your grief and all of the conflicting emotions that come with it can be transformational. By telling
yourself the truth, your mind, your body, and your spirit are all
able to do their hard work. You
may feel your heart is broken
but actually it's working just fine
if you just allow it to feel whatever it feels - despair, anguish,
regret, even joy and gratitude in
the reminiscing.

> *You may feel your*
> *heart is broken but*
> *actually it's working*
> *just fine if you*
> *just allow it to feel*
> *whatever it feels-*
> *despair, anguish,*
> *regret, even joy in*
> *the reminiscing.*

Says Madeleine L'Engle:

Those who believe they believe
in God, but without passion
in the heart, without anguish of mind, without uncertainty,
without doubt, and even at times without despair, believe in
the idea of God, and not in God himself.

Another word for this is spiritual by-passing. It occurs when
we try to by-pass our real emotions and try to avoid the mess-
iness of human living. It's hiding behind a kind of religiosity.
Spiritual by-passing assumes that if we are spiritual enough,
if we pray, meditate, and/or study scripture enough we will

somehow be above the challenges that come with being human. But we must be willing to sit in the dark unknown for a while and befriend what we find there. A descent is necessary before transformation can come about. This is painful but necessary for rebirth. It is during these dark times that the best prayers are prayed - the most authentic prayers.[16] And I'm pretty sure those are the only ones God really wants anyway.

Says Jan L. Richardson in her beautiful book *In the Sanctuary of Women: A Companion for Reflection and Prayer:*

> *There are prayers whispered, wailed, shouted, groaned; prayers sung and laughed and wept and dreamed. There are prayers of stillness and of silence, prayers in the breath and in the belly, prayers in the beating heart and in the space between the beats. There are prayers.[17]*

Yes.

The incomparable theologian Frederick Buechner (1926-2022) wrote about his boyhood experience of losing his father to suicide. He said he was telling this part of his life story at a men's retreat and afterwards a man came up to him and said, "You've been a good steward of your pain." Buechner said he was taken aback by the comment and had to mull it over in his mind and heart for a period of time.[18] Suffering, of course, is universal and I guess that statement would mean different things to different people. For me, I think that being a good steward of my pain means I want to live out my life with an intent to love the way Nicole did in order to honor her life in that way. To live with this purpose and a kind of quiet integrity and wholeness as best I can. To continue living with an open heart that allows room for joy but also risks more sorrow. To believe that we are somehow enlarged in the waiting and the wondering. Because I think maybe being a "good steward of your pain" is about the best any of us could ever aspire to.

Chapter Twenty-One

Above All, Trust in the Slow Work of God

(Pierre Teilhard de Chardin)

It's the first of June, school is out for the summer and the sun is high in the sky. A little Toyota truck zooms by and I think of Nicole. Only a few months away from getting her driver's license, she never had the chance to buy her dream vehicle - a small pick up truck - so much an expression of her personality. I can picture her driving down to the cliffs of Santa Cruz, surf board in the back, wind in her hair, ready for the waves. Now - a dream deferred. Do they have oceans in heaven? Or dream vehicles?

On this day here on Planet Earth, I've arranged to take two of Nicole's friends, Scarlett and Ava, to lunch at a local cafe. I've made up goodie bags for them to open on the plane when they vacation together this summer. It's something I used to do for my grandkids when they were smaller and not yet phone addicted. In addition to small bags of candy and popcorn I've packed mini Etch-a-Sketches and books with word and letter puzzles. It's all in good fun and the girls are so pleased. MacKenzie and Natalie (who the friend group has fully embraced as their little sister) have joined this little party and there is a lot of laughter around the table. The girls are full of summer plans:

I once told Nic, "Every summer has a story." But in this summer's story, the girl who would be my protagonist would not appear.

cheer camp, bonfires at the beach, and endless sleepovers and parties. I am caught up in the happiness for them but of course a corner of my heart is badly aching. I once told Nic, "Every summer has a story." But in this summer's story the girl who would be my protagonist will not appear.

Over the course of time that Nicole has been gone MacKenzie has hosted so many dinners for Nicole's friends. The beautiful dining area is now a place of celebration and love and friendship and good food. Bright candles are flickering, the table is set with care, dishes and glasses sparkle, and laughter drowns out the sounds of silverware clinking.

The yearbook staff at Nicole's high school did a dedication page for her the year she would have been a Sophomore. It read:

Nicole Keller was the type of person who lights up a room the second she steps into it. She was such a genuine soul with a glowing spirit and continues to inspire thousands every single day. She was kind, outgoing, fun, beautiful, and one of the funniest girls ever. She was loved by everyone she met and was always there for everybody no matter what. She was loyal, she was loving, she was caring, she was just amazing. She could be in the worst situation and still be the most positive person in the room. She would never focus on herself and only on how others would be affected...... She will forever be loved immensely and missed like crazy.

My heart opened up with gratitude, love, and grief when I read these words. The page said to me: **Nicole Keller was here. And her life mattered.** And it matters still.

As Frederick Buechner says, "....whatever the world choses to do later on, it can never so much as lay a hand on the having-beenness of this time."[19]

May her memory be a blessing.

Epilogue

Since Nicole has been gone so many people have reached out to form memorials in her honor. A little tree was donated to grow and stand tall on the campus of Nicole's elementary school where MacKenzie works. What a blessing for my daughter to see this beautiful tree each day in honor of her child. My husband and I were also given a tree for our garden- and it will provide us beautiful blossoms each spring, a reminder of renewal and restoration.

A generous donation was made in Nicole's name to Big Basin State Park where Nicole and I spent that lovely day.

After Nicole passed Mack continued to have Bible studies in her home for some of Nic's friends. Exactly one year from the last Good Friday when Nicole wrote that love letter to God after her chemo had ended, under gray skies on a very blustery and stormy late afternoon on a beach in California, Anni, one of the beautiful girls from the group, made her way out into the Pacific Ocean with her pastor and was baptized.

Soon a picnic table to commemorate our girl will be installed in a state park in a beautiful redwood grove that overlooks the ocean. It will be a lasting place for our family to gather. My husband has already said he wants to celebrate all of his birthdays there.

And last, interestingly, there seem to be a lot of people walking around now with tiny little hearts tattooed on their ankles.

A Blessing

for Those Who Grieve and Wonder

As time goes by may the questions
lose their bite and sting.

May you have the courage to walk alongside
them and find grace and peace for the journey.

Appendix A

Journaling Pages

1. Did you or do you have a grandmother with whom you had or have a relationship? What was or is that like? Are there words of wisdom that she passed on to you?

2. How does prayer or meditation play a part in your life? That is, do you pray and/or meditate and what is that like?

3. If Christianity is your tradition , how would you describe God the Father? What informs your thoughts/ feelings about Him?

4. Do you have a positive connection with nature and animals? If so, describe. What are the settings and feelings that come to mind? What are the benefits?

5. Looking back, do you have "ebenezers" or times when you can point to when you felt God or a Higher Power was near or taking care of you?

6. Write a letter to this Higher Power that reflects your questions about the loss of your loved one.

_____

_____

_____

_____

_____

_____

_____

_____

_____

_____

_____

_____

7. Finish this sentence: I wish........

....

....

....

....

....

....

....

....

....

....

....

....

8. Write about your lost loved one: The thing I most remember about him/her is .....and/or write a letter to him/her and if you wish paste a photo here.

....

....

....

....

....

....

....

....

....

....

....

....

9. Finish this sentence: Grief is.......

....

....

....

....

....

....

....

....

....

....

....

....

....

10. Can you point to any meaningful music in your life that evokes pain, peace, or joy?

....

....

....

....

....

....

....

....

....

....

....

....

11. Finish this sentence: Even though.....

....

....

....

....

....

....

....

....

....

....

....

....

12. Does your culture include special funeral rituals?
Describe your experience.

13. What are your beliefs about an afterlife?

14. What does "being a good steward of your pain" mean to you?

15. Do you have a trusted professional you can speak with to help with your pain? Do you have open-hearted friends who will listen and share with you? What can you do to take care of yourself?

Appendix B

From Psalm 139

You have searched me, Lord

and you know me.

You know when I sit and when I rise;

you perceive my thoughts from afar.

You discern my going out

and my lying down;

you are familiar with all of my ways.

Before a word is on my tongue

you, Lord, know it completely.

You hem me in behind and before,

and you lay your hand upon me.

Such knowledge is too wonderful for me,

too lofty for me to to attain.

Where can I go from your Spirit?

Where can I flee from your presence?

If I go up to the heavens you are there.

If I make my bed in the depths you are there.

If I rise on the wings of the dawn,

if I settle on the far side of the sea,

even there your hand will guide me,

your right hand will hold me fast.

If I say, "Surely the darkness will hide me

and the light become night around me,"

even the darkness will not be dark to you;

the night will shine like the day,

for darkness is as light to you.

For you created my inmost being;

you knit me together in my mother's womb.

I praise you because I am fearfully and wonderfully made;

your words are wonderful, I know that full well.

My frame was not hidden from you when I was made

in the secret place, when I was woven together

in the depths of the earth.

Your eyes saw my unformed body;

all the days ordained for me

were written in your book before one of them came to be.

How precious to me are your thoughts, God!

How vast the sum of them!

Were I to count them,

they would outnumber the grains of sand-

when I awake, I am still with you.

. . . .

Search me, God, and know my heart;

test me and know my anxious thoughts.

See if there is any offensive way in me,

and lead me in the way everlasting.

(italics mine)

Endnotes

1   Keelin O'Donohue, "Fetal Microchimerism and Maternal Health During and After Pregnancy" National Library of Medicine: Obstetric Medicine, December 1, 2008

2   Laura Sanders, "Children's Cells Live on in Their Mothers" Science News, May 10, 2015

3   Richard Rohr, *Yes, And....* (Cincinnati: Franciscan Media, 2013), 20

4   Kat Armas, *Sacred Belonging* (Grand Rapids: Brazos Press, 2023), 20,29

5   Phillip Yancy, *Disappointment with God* (Grand Rapids: Zondervan, 1988), 263

6   Tish Harrison Warren, *Prayer in the Night: For Those Who Work or Watch or Weep* (Downers Grove: Intervarsity Press, 2021), 27

7   Gregory Boyle, *Barking to the Choir: The Power of Radical Kinship* (New York: Simon and Schuster, 2017), 112, 113

8   Anne Lamott, *Stitches* (New York: Riverhead Books, 2013), 39

9   Anne Lamott, "Living the Unremarkable Moments" The Washington Post, September 2, 2024

10   The John S. Randall Peace Page, November 20, 2024

11   Eugene Peterson, *The Message* (Colorado Springs: NavPress, 1995), 11

12   Mark Buchanan, *Your God is Too Safe* (Grand Rapids: Multnomah Books, 2001), 145

13   Richard Rohr, *Everything Belongs* (New York: The Crossroad Publishing Company, 2003) 143,144

14   John Marzluff and Tony Angell, *Gifts of the Crow* (New York: Atria Paperback, 2013), 137-139

15   Mary Frances O'Connor, *The Grieving Body* (New York: HarperCollins, 2025), 2-4

16   Christine Valters Paintner, *A Midwinter God* (Notre Dame: Soren Books, 2024), 28

17   Jan L. Richardson, *In the Sanctuary of Women: A Companion for Reflection and Prayer* (Nashville: Upper Room Books, 2010), 11

18   Frederick Büechner, *A Crazy Holy Grace: The Healing Power of Pain and Memory* (Grand Rapids: Zondervan, 2017), 16

19   Frederick Büechner, *Listening to Your Life* (New York: HarperCollins,1992), 277

Grateful Acknowledgments

I think nothing makes a mother happier than when people are kind to her children.

Thank you from the bottom of my heart to all of the people in the Scotts Valley community and beyond who loved and supported my daughter, MacKenzie, through this trial. It was a double whammy for me to see both my daughter and my granddaughter endure this crucible.

I am eternally grateful.

To MacKenzie's dear friends: Stephanie, Kelly, Sarah, Jacqui, Mendy, Angelique. To all of the sweet women in her Bible study who prayed and prayed; to Michelle for your never ending generosity, faithfulness, and love. To Elia for the helicopter ride and all of your generosity.

Thank you Jordan for the driving lessons and thank you Maddie for choreographing such a beautiful dance.

To all of Nicole's friends who are too numerous to name, but here are just a few: Maddie, Scarlett, Julia, Ava, Giuliana, Collin, Tea, Kennan, Riya, Penny.

Thank you to the Lyons and Siegle families for the beautiful trees.

To the Porter and Keller families for your love and support.

Many thanks to the Hall family, the Marsh family, the Svalya family.

Thank you for all of the clinicians who helped: to the whole staff at Kidwise-Dr. Walker, nurses Ally and Rhio; to Dr. Pribnow; to Dr. Goldman; to nurses Mama T, Julie, and Becky; to Nicole's real physical therapist Amanda; to my grief counselor Veronica.

Thank you to the kind ladies at St. Francis Soup Kitchen.

Thank you to all of my friends for your open hearts and listening ears:

To Margaret, Sandy, Phyllis, Mary Lynn, and Caryl. Thank you Dawn for your creative advice.

To my fellow sojourners in Theodyssey: Pat, Kay, and Sara.

Thank you Christine for all your love and generosity.

Thank you Darci who knows: If you want to walk fast walk alone; if you want to walk far walk together.

Thank you Pam for always providing a safe harbor.

Deb - love you long time girl.

Thank you everyone at Aptos United Methodist Church. Because as our pastor, Gabe, says: "Methodists don't just GO to church, they DO church." And you sure did.

Thank you to our whole crazy, fun, and loving family - we carry on, we stick together:

To Kim and Steph for making the trip; to Clyde and Judy for your amazing generosity; to Aunt Becky, seamstress extraordinaire; to the Guncles for just *everything*; to Nana Trish and Papa Dan; to the Frankulls; to the Williams family.

Blessings on all of my precious grandchildren: may God protect you and show you the way forward. You each made Nicole's life happier.

To Carl for always being there for me and for being the best Poppa ever to our girl.

And always - to the Cord of Three.

Most of all to MacKenzie, my beloved daughter. Your strength and steadfast faith are an inspiration to me.

About the Author

 Victoria Cull holds advanced degrees in theology, special education, and counseling. A longtime educator and counselor in California's public schools, she is also the author of *Positive Visualizations: Solution-Based Strategies to Empower Students.* She lives on California's central coast with her husband, Carl, and their dog, Bobby McGee. She is the grateful mother of three and grandmother of six. She enjoys gardening, swimming, hiking, spending time with equines, and volunteering at her local library.